T0194203

Wisdom Flows from the Heart

Inspiration for the Heart & Soul!

Pouring out from the heart with
expressions of wisdom inspired by God!

Revive, Refresh, Restore, Renew

Adalia Raye Gwaltney

authorHOUSE®

AuthorHouse™
1663 Liberty Drive
Bloomington, IN 47403
www.authorhouse.com
Phone: 1-800-839-8640

First published by AuthorHouse   5/17/2011

ISBN: 978-1-4567-6120-2 (e)
ISBN: 978-1-4567-6121-9 (sc)

Library of Congress Control Number: 2011906510

Printed in the United States of America

Any people depicted in stock imagery provided by Thinkstock are models, and such images are being used for illustrative purposes only. Certain stock imagery © Thinkstock.

This book is printed on acid-free paper.

Unless otherwise noted, all scripture quotations in this publication are from the Holy Bible (Public Domain), King James Version (KJV).

Contents

This special message is dedicated to the adult and young adult population, who know that they are still a work in progress being restored and renewed by God—spiritually, mentally, and physically.

Wisdom resteth in the heart of him that hath understanding: but that which is in the midst of fools is made known.

—Proverbs 14:33

Foreword

Ms. Adalia Raye Gwaltney, author of *Wisdom Flows from the Heart: Inspiration for the Heart & Soul*, is a woman of God. She is using her life's experiences, the good and the challenges, to assist teens on the brink of adulthood and adults to trust in God. Ms. Gwaltney shares her story through the journeys and tells how each journey affords her the opportunity to trust and depend on God even the more. The journey is the mechanism used by God in preparation for each level of her journey. She shares that a repeat journey is an indication that a lesson has not been learned.

In the book, Ms. Gwaltney says, "When I feel depressed, lonely, or discouraged, I pray... I began to feel His presence, and the taste was bursting with flavors of blessings, and my life has changed for the good."

Wisdom Flows from the Heart: Inspiration for the Heart & Soul is an important book. It should inspire the reader to seek and to search for a closer relationship with God through His Son, Jesus Christ.

Ms. Gwaltney continues her life's walk with God by reading the Word daily, and by participating in Bible class and Bible school. Ms. Gwaltney is ever searching the scriptures for revelation and direction from God.

Ms. Gwaltney will reach the world in her eloquent writing style. Her writings will ultimately become an integral component of Christian ministry.

Juanita Berry
Bridge Street AWME Church
Brooklyn, New York 11221

Preface

A Holy Calling

It is important that I give honor to God, because the Holy Spirit inspired me to write this book concerning the movement of God in the Millennium. His mighty working power is still manifesting in the lives of men, women, and children throughout the world today. I thank God for using me to experience His wondrous power and transforming me from the state of being a sinner to a saint (Christian). I was a sinner living in darkness, rebelling and enjoying the pleasures of this world, and I needed a change in my lifestyle. I made a decision to accept Jesus Christ as my Savior. Accepting Christ began the renewing process of my mind, and my fleshly desires gradually diminished over time as God called me to service. As a servant, I became obedient to God and began living according to the principles of the Word of God, which conditioned me to live a holy and virtuous life. The Bible tells us that out of the heart of man flow the issues of life, and when the Spirit of God told me that I had a heart of holiness, I was commissioned to labor for the Kingdom of God. This book describes the transformation process that I experienced as I matured as a Christian, studying the Word of God and making prayer and worship a priority in my life. Overall, I submitted my will to God, and now I have a more intimate relationship with our Heavenly Father. Everything you are about to read was born out of my life experiences of tests, trials, and victories. I pray that you will be inspired, encouraged, and educated by this special message of love and inspiration. I believe that the Spirit of God will come upon you and release refreshment to nurture your spirit, soul, and body to begin your journey to labor for the Kingdom of God.

Acknowledgments

I thank God for the love and patience of my mother, Sophia L. Gwaltney, and my grandmother, Lucille Hook. The Lord blessed them to be women of substance who have consistently labored in prayer for our family's salvation and deliverance. I thank God for my sisters and brothers in Christ for their love, prayers, and support. To God be the glory for sustaining me to complete this spiritual workmanship.

Introduction

When God begins to work on you, He starts with the heart, which is the most sensitive organ in the body. He is constantly shaping and molding broken vessels; no matter who you are or what you are currently doing in your life, God loves you. If He cleaned me up, I know that God can do the same for you, because He is the potter and we are the clay. These words of inspiration and wisdom have been spoken to audiences of various backgrounds and in different religious settings. Many were transformed and encouraged as a result of the spoken word, which brought about a closer relationship with God.

This section is an overview of the topics that are listed in the table of contents, for the purpose of helping the reader understand each part of the book.

Faith Walk

When you come to the realization that God loves you and He is the source of your strength, no matter what situation you may encounter, you can always trust that He will come to your rescue. When you develop that kind of faith and trust in God, there are no limits to what He can do in your life. He is a loving and forgiving God, and He expects us to develop a heart of compassion, so that we will have the strength to forgive others. Whatever your heart desires to know, God will not hold back any secrets. The Lord will reveal secrets things to you when you are prepared to accept the truth concerning your life, in your walk of faith and trust in Him.

Draw Near to God

Life situations can draw us near to God whether they are good or bad experiences; He is always available. He hears our cry, and shouts of praise and thanksgiving. God knows everything about us, because we are made in His image. He will heal your broken heart and mend your physical and mental wounds. God will forgive you for your mistakes, because He is a loving and merciful Father. You don't have to travel across the world to find our Heavenly Father, because He is present everywhere, and I know Him to be the only true and living God. Draw near to God and be a witness to His mighty working power, and don't be afraid to let His divine will be done in your life.

Anchored in the Lord

There is an urgency to be anchored in the Lord, because Jesus is soon to return. We ought to give God honor and praise, because He is the keeper of our soul. We need to thank God for Jesus dying on the cross and redeeming us from the curse of sin and death. When you make a decision to depend totally on the Lord, He will give you the peace that surpasses all understanding. God loves us, and you can be assured that you can trust Him to restore and change your way of living. When you have a better understanding of who you are in Christ Jesus, you will realize that it is good to give God the glory for being on your side. Make a decision to anchor yourself in the Lord and study the Bible. God is able to keep you from falling and set you back on track.

More Than a Conqueror

In life you may not win every battle, but knowing that you fought the good fight of faith makes you more than a conqueror. You don't have to fight your battles alone, because God is your strong tower, and He will defend you in all situations. If you have experienced more defeats than wins, don't let it be a discouragement, but a lesson in learning to develop strategies. Keep your mind set on winning and never give up during your struggles, because you will survive the battle. God is on your side, and He can defeat any giant in your life that comes up against you. So stand still and see the salvation of the Lord, and you will have the victory!

Deliver Me from Myself

In life you may experience the feelings of being rejected, humiliated, oppressed, and depressed, but God is able to heal and mend your wounds, regardless of any situation that you encounter. It is easy to become overwhelmed when you have a lot of issues confronting you and try to handle them on your own, but it is wise to prioritize your matters to determine what is more important and beneficial for your well-being. Sometimes, we get tired of living the single life and make a commitment to get married, but never marry for selfish reasons, because it can cause a lot of despair in the future. Getting married for the wrong reasons will get you into trouble. You may experience so much turmoil in your relationship that you'll need God to deliver you from yourself. It is critical that you ask God for guidance concerning the individual whom you intend to spend your life with, because you can a make mistake in listening to your mind and not your heart. Take time to examine your thoughts to determine if love motivates you to get married or whether it is an overwhelming desire for the flesh. For some people, it may be both love and lust, but if you are just hungry for the moment, I encourage you to take inventory of your desires of the flesh. Marriage is a commitment, a union, and a fellowship that God instituted, and there is nothing wrong with getting godly counsel or help from a professional if you are having problems. We have our own minds to make choices, but be aware: there is a battle going on in our minds daily. So don't be deceived; be wise and let God direct your path.

Part One
Faith Walk

The Gift Box of Love

My heart is like a gift box wrapped with ribbons of love and filled only with presents that I want stored away. When I am sad, I reach in for happiness. When I feel fearful, I reach for courage. When I am weak, I reach for strength. When I feel like I've lost my confidence, I reach deep down for faith. When I feel like the world is on my shoulders, I reach out my arms to God to lift up my spirit and to touch my soul! The Almighty renews my heart and rewraps my ribbons with a greater glow of love!

From the Streets to the Church

There is a saying about people who grew up in urban communities that many still call the ghetto, but if you research the word you will discover that it did not originate in America! It was labeled as such because of the standards of the community being in a state of poverty, with inadequate housing, lack of health care, high crime rates, educational problems, low income, unemployment, and so forth. The list can go on and on about getting just enough to live on a daily basis. In fact, if you were in the no-income or low-income bracket, you qualified for government assistance, and a lot of cheese came with that package during the seventies and eighties. This I know because some of our good neighbors gave our family some of their cheese and butter. I must say that the problem of people being in lack still exists today, throughout some of the richest countries in the world. I often wonder why. I was born in the year 1960, and when I became old enough to understand my surroundings and things happening within my household, I remember living in an economically deprived community.

Fortunately, there was hope for deprived communities as changes began to occur in the political arena over the years. Great leaders struggled and fought for justice and equality, even before the sixties. There were concerns about urban renewal, housing developments, cleaner streets, better services for underprivileged people, jobs, safe streets, etc., and the word *ghetto* should have been called the new and improved community. Yes, many changes occurred to improve the living conditions for the people, but the gang fighting, drugs, prostitution, corruption, and high school dropouts were still the norm, along with other ills in society. I believe that the pressures of society contributed to a lot of hostility amongst the people, which may have caused many to become angry, but the key to the entire confusion was the church. The church was a place of refuge where people from all lifestyles were welcome in fellowship. I thank God for prayer and unity within my family because that was the place to be on Sundays. Whenever you needed to get away from the outside world, walking into a church service helped to block out the commotion that existed outside the walls of the church. The church was more serene and sacred because it was all about Jesus. Amen!

However, I discovered that there was an awful projection of how some people in society viewed folks in the ghetto. Someone or a group of individuals came up with this cliché: "You can take a person out of the ghetto, but you can't take the ghetto out of the person." I understand this cliché to mean an individual living in a new environment with the same habits and conduct. Some people may have been considered as being in a certain class, but one should never underestimate a person's ability or intellect. Some great people have come out of some of the worst communities that you can imagine and have become successful! Yes, and I just want to testify, when I discovered my gifts and talents, my strengths and weaknesses, I knew that "I can do all things through Christ which strengthened me." (Philippians: 4:13) Praise the Lord! We need to take advantage of the opportunities that were not available to minorities in the past and pursue our goals. How far have we really come to see vast changes for minorities from during the time that I was born until now, the Millennium?

I've witnessed a continuation of ups and downs, shifts, and twists and turns. A number of minorities have become successful because they took advantage of the opportunities in the areas of medicine, music, technology, sports, government, and education, just to name a few, but there are still obstacles in these fields today. People still have issues that have not been addressed or resolved. We are still living in the same nightmare of the ills of society, even with the mighty computer, medical breakthroughs, and global awareness, but thank God for the church. We can still go into the house of God to worship in accord with our brothers and sisters, to lift up our voices and praise the Lord. Amen! More so, I thank God for the great change in the White House. For the first time in the history of America, an African American was elected for the position of president of the United States in 2008. However, even though his position has a four-year term, the effort was progress on a greater scale for minorities in 2008. Yes we can, and yes it came to pass, but in reality, there is never a dull moment! I encourage you to make a decision to fulfill your purpose in life and don't waste time, because the clock is ticking!

Special nugget: If you are hanging around with people who are set in their ways, have bad intentions, and are still dwelling on the past, distance yourself and try to associate with people who are talking about great expectations for the future!

Part Two
Draw Near to God

Never a Dull Moment

Each day of our life we are faced with some type of challenge or experience that causes us to change our plans and strategies, but there is a reason for everything. Do you often wonder if God has something to do with your course of action? Think about it; are you really in the will of God? One minute things are calm, and the next minute there is some type of havoc. I have discovered that you have to fight the good fight of faith, because Satan is always seeking whom he may devour. We need to learn from our experiences, whether good or bad, because they prepare us for greater challenges in life. I've found, that there are many solutions to handling our problems, and the world system certainly has answers and ways to solve them. Some are through counseling, mediation, medication, drugs, alcohol, and the Internet. Which would you choose? When I was young, I was taught to call on the name of Jesus, and to pray and believe that God is the problem solver.

I encourage you to escape from the streets and find refuge in the house of God, the church! It is time for you to stir up your intellect and read books that have some substance. It is also good to read the Bible and learn the Word of God to find out what the Bible is all about. Make an effort to purpose in your mind to live a humble life, speak the Word of God, and take the Word back to the streets and tell somebody about Jesus, because He is coming back for the church! So, rise and shine for Jesus; the moment has come for you to rise and shine for Jesus! Don't let the evil ways of the world outweigh the goodness in you. When the storm clouds in your life begin to fall like the rain from the sky, pray for peace in the midst of your storm. When you feel like you are drowning and sinking deep into sin, keep your head above the water and look toward Heaven and call on the name of Jesus! Let the Word of God be your anchor to pull you out of the rough waters and to place your feet on solid ground. You will proclaim that Jesus Christ is Lord, and He will prepare you to go into the water of spiritual sustenance to be baptized in the name of the Father, and the Son, and the Holy Ghost. Psalm 42:8 says, "Yet the Lord will command his lovingkindness in the daytime, and in the night his song shall be with me, and my prayer unto the God of my life." I am convinced that prayer is not a ritual, but a lifestyle, and I am a witness for the Lord!

Do You Know Where You Come From?

Some of the best-kept secrets are in the family. You might say, What kind of secrets? Well, they are the secrets of your family history. Some people have been able to trace their generations all the way back to their ancestral roots, while others like myself have only traced back to my great-grandmother, because everybody else is a mystery and a well-kept secret. I have an opportunity to do the research, and it is good when someone knows about his or her family history and can share it with the next generation. I understand now why it is good to have family reunions, because they are certainly a way to get to know your relatives and heritage. I never had the opportunity to ask my grandmother about her grandparents, which would have been a third generation, but the thought never crossed my mind. I am guilty of not having made the attempt to find out about our family history while my grandmother was still living. I should have taken the time to find out, but I was busy trying to enjoy growing up in a wild community. My mother told me that her grandmother's name was Elizabeth Boyd, but she could not remember her great-grandmother's name. I was happy to know that our family is a mix of Indian and African.

My mother was born in the 1930s, and my grandmother was born in the year 1907. Of course, my great-grandmother was born in the late 1800s in Orangeburg, South Carolina. Therefore, when I begin to think about the 1800s, 1700s, 1600s, 1500s, and so forth down the years, I can't fathom my ancestors' way of life, but slavery was definitely present. Plantations were active and wooden houses and shacks were standing, with stone ovens, kettles, cast iron pans, candles, and oil burners. The bathroom facilities were known as the outhouse, which was a distance from the house somewhere in the woods. I can name many other things that were present during the time of slavery, and the list can go on into the thousands. I was not born during that era, but knowing the history of slavery and things that occurred during that era is certainly an overwhelming feeling. Most important, I thank God that the women in my family survived the course of time, so that my generation could exist. The men of the family who were part of the process survived the humiliation of being treated without respect and kept hope alive that my generation was destined to arrive. Thank you, Jesus! I thank God for the generations of men and women who gave birth in my family lineage, because it was the grace of God, the hymns of Zion, and all of the men and women of valor that contributed to the escape from slavery to safety, and on to freedom. Praise the Lord!

The story of my father's family is no different from my mother's. I knew my grandfather, James Gwaltney, but not my great-grandfather. Secrets, secrets, and secrets … my family is full of secrets, but thank God that my mother had the opportunity to meet my grandfather. The last name that we inherited just happens to be part of a well-known company that used to market meat products, called "Gwaltney." My question is, "What is the mystery behind the Gwaltney family of Smithfield, Virginia?" My grandparents' family are from Virginia, but what happened with that story? Was it really Meadville, Virginia, or Smithfield? This issue is still a mystery to me, although my father tried to explain some things concerning the Gwaltney family and our connection to the name. I'm still trying to find out what happened to my inheritance. Was my family eligible to receive a portion—or better yet, entitled to the stock?

It is evident that the name still carries some kind of reputation, because it's still active today. My family may have been left out of the Gwaltney inheritance, but thank God we are included in the heritage of Jesus. Yes, we have received a greater inheritance from God because of His Son Jesus Christ. The Word of God says in Romans 8:16–17, "The Spirit itself beareth witness with our spirit, that we are the children of God: And if children, then heirs; heirs of God, and joint-heirs with Christ; if so be that we suffer with him, that we may be also glorified together." Now, I believe God about my relationship with Jesus, and that settles it! Therefore, it does not matter that my family was not included in the reaping of the Gwaltney harvest, because we have a greater heritage. We have a glorious heritage. We have eternal life through Jesus Christ our Lord and Savior. We have the opportunity to praise the Lord and thank God because all is not lost, but gained, and there is no secret what God can do! My question to you is, "Do you know where you come from?"

A Familiar Journey

I am no different from you; the salty tears of sorrow that roll down my face come from a pair of brown eyes. What color are yours? When the sun beams down on my brown skin, it makes me one shade darker. What shade does the sun change your complexion to? When I pray, I kneel down with my hands close together and my head bowed down, ready to pray to God out loud or in silence. How do you pray? I made a few wrong turns down several different roads that only led me to a life of deception, confusion, pain, and temporary happiness. Have you ever been down a road similar to mine?

Well, this is what happened to me, after that long journey down those crooked roads: I fell down on my knees and began to see a straight and narrow path that led me to the road of redemption. I met Jesus at the crossroads, and I surrendered to Him. He washed my sins away. He guided me in a direction that gave me hope for all of the doubts in my life, love for my broken heart, comfort for my sorrows, faith to trust in God, and strength for the new journey to live a Christian life. I also knew at that moment why my tears were salty, and why the sun's radiance gave me a new complexion. Jesus was trying to show me that my tears of sorrow will be changed to tears of joy; and the new shade of my complexion was a sign of being made new with the blood of Christ. Glory to God! The falling down on my knees was an indication of how I should pray to God and ask for forgiveness for every sin that I had ever committed. I thank God because it was His divine will that I made it this far today.

If by chance you are in doubt about the road that you should journey down, just ask God to show you the way and to give you the wisdom to be able to handle the challenges that you will encounter on your new journey. I encourage you to ask in the name of Jesus! James 4:10 says, "Humble yourselves in the sight of the Lord, and he shall lift you up."

Labor in Love, for God Is Love

"For God is not unrighteous to forget your work and labour of love, which ye have shewed toward his name, in that ye have ministered to the saints, and do minister." (Hebrews 6:10) Beloved, this scripture is not referring to the twenty-five or thirty years that you have labored for your employer and how you are going to be compensated when you retire. Neither is it referring to your efforts to keep your house clean to impress people, and it is certainly not referring to your first and only good deed. No! The Word of God is referring to your labor for the Kingdom of God in which you are doing the will of God. This kind of labor requires you to love your neighbor as you love yourself and to help those who are less fortunate than you. I believe that it is good to encourage people with a word from the Lord, especially when they are in a state of sorrow, because everybody experiences moments of weakness.

I am convinced that some people may say that it is a struggle to love someone who despises you and will do anything to harm you. Do you know that God has the remedy for your struggle? The Word of God tells us to pray for those who despitefully use you. Beloved, we ought to obey instructions. We need to show compassion to people who are hurting, but how can you show compassion when you are hurting also and trying to smile through your words of wisdom? It is a struggle and a task! However, I found out that when you encourage people with words of inspiration, it helps to boost their self-esteem, and you will gain a sense of relief knowing that you made a difference in someone's life. God expects us to love one another, because God is love and love is the fruit of the spirit. In the book of Galatians 5:22–24, the Word of God says, "But the fruit of the Spirit is love, joy, peace, longsuffering, gentleness, goodness, faith, Meekness, temperance: against such there is no law. And they that are Christ's have crucified the flesh with the affections and lusts." We need to examine ourselves on a daily basis to see if the fruits of the spirit are being manifested in our lives. Sometimes we behave like the tangible fruit, such as pears, apples, oranges, mangos, and bananas, just waiting for our season to ripen or hanging on the tree becoming rotten!

We should examine ourselves and take inventory to compare ourselves with how these types of fruits grow, because we need to grow also, but spiritually. This type of fruit grows on branches and needs to be pruned. They need sun, water, air, and constant nurturing in order to grow. If you think about these elements in nature, you will realize that our body requires nurturing also. We need sun, water, and air, as well as other nutrients for the body to sustain us. The trees that bear these fruits are deeply rooted in the ground and take some time to grow. I believe that we need to grow while waiting for our season to excel and become successful, but many of us are in a rush to branch out. Jesus said in John 15:1–2, "I am the true vine, and my Father is the husbandman. Every branch in me that beareth not fruit he taketh away: and every branch that beareth fruit, he purgeth it, that it may bring forth more fruit." Amen! What kind of fruit are you producing? Let me remind you that we are the church (the body of Christ), and we have many members, but are one body.

We need to come together as one and let the enemy know that we will not be defeated, because there is power in the name of Jesus. We must demonstrate our love and compassion toward others. I have witnessed through the testimonies of overcomers that God is on our side. Psalm 34:8 says, "O taste and see that the LORD is good: blessed is the man that trusteth in him." Beloved, I trust and believe that God is my personal Savior, and I am a living testimony! It took a long time for me to realize that throughout my life, God has been with me all the time. He saved me from all of the "dangerous adventures" in my life. God has blessed me with confidence, faith, and the ability to love and pray for my enemies. I am a witness for the Lord! When I feel depressed, lonely, or discouraged, I pray and ask God for comfort, and I get good results. Whenever my problems or burdens become too hard for me to solve, I pray and ask God to step into my situation and to order my steps, and I get good results. I made a decision a long time ago to trust in God, and I began to feel His presence. The taste was bursting with flavors of blessings, and my life has changed for the good.

Beloved, I believe that God has something magnificent for you. Make a decision to trust and believe that you can get good results through prayer. It worked for me, and today I am a witness for the Lord, striving to bear good fruit and laboring for the Kingdom of God. Purpose in your mind to walk by faith and not by sight in all situations!

Part Three
Anchored in the Lord

Comforter in the Midnight Hour

Jesus is a friend of mine, and there is something about His name. Is Jesus your friend? Is He there in the midnight hour when you are in despair? Has He washed your sins away? We often hear "That at the name of Jesus every knee should bow, of things in heaven, and things in earth, and things under the earth; And that every tongue should confess that Jesus Christ is Lord, to the glory of God the Father." (Philippians 2:10–11) Whose report do you believe? Are you going to walk by faith or by sight? Are you willing to bow down in the name of Jesus? I encourage you to have faith and trust in God in every area of your life. Amen! When we begin to sing the song "Silent Night," some people really look forward to a silent night—a night to sleep in peace and not worry about having nightmares and waking up in a cold sweat.

We need to feed our spirit by reading the Bible daily and listening to the Word of God as well. It is good to watch television programs or movies that are inspirational and have some substance that will contribute to your growth and development in today's society. Hello, somebody! People have a choice to watch, hear, or read whatever they desire, but most of what we are exposed to on a daily basis are revisited in our dreams. We should be careful about what we allow to sink into our hearts and minds, because it can contribute to negative or positive dreams. I always look forward to experiencing sweet dreams that make me sleep like a baby, but some dreams just don't turn out the way we expect. Guess what? I know that I have the option to wake up in the middle of the night and call on the name of Jesus or roll over and return to the undesirable dream. What will you do? Whom will you call on to feel safe and secure after waking up in a cold sweat?

Beloved, I am persuaded that while we are asleep God continues to breathe life into us, and we ought to be thankful for His grace and mercy. The Bible tells us that weeping may endure for a night, but joy will come in the morning. So, when we rise up early, we ought to praise God for the dawning of the day. We need to be polite and thank the Lord whether the sun is shining, the rain is falling, or cold and dreary. We still should have praise in our mouth, even though the weather affects how we think and feel. I believe that Christians forget about the light that is still flickering inside of us, and that is the light of Jesus. Your heart can still be filled with joy regardless of how bad things are or appear to be.

Sometimes we need to look at the bright side of things, because God will send someone to encourage you and to remind you that the Holy Spirit will comfort you.

I believe that when you call on the name of Jesus, there will be peace in your situation. I know from experience that when you put your trust in God, He will be like a bridge over troubled waters. He will come to your rescue, even when you are down to your last dime or drowning and sinking into sin. Jesus said, "Come unto me, all ye that labour and are heavy laden, and I will give you rest. Take my yoke upon you, and learn of me; for I am meek and lowly in heart: and ye shall find rest unto your souls. For my yoke is easy, and my burden is light." (Matthew 11:28–30) I encourage you to speak to your situation and say, Peace be still, in the name of Jesus!

The Strait Gate

"Enter ye in at the strait gate: for wide is the gate, and broad is the way, that leadeth to destruction, and many there be which go in thereat: Because strait is the gate, and narrow is the way, which leadeth unto life, and few there be that find it." (Matthew 7:13–14)

I used to enjoy the things of the world that kept me in bondage, and I never acknowledged that God knew everything that I was doing. In fact, I devoted 85 percent of my time enjoying the things of the world and 15 percent in recognizing God as the source of my life. When I began to pay attention to what God was doing in my life, I became confident. I was taught to pray for protection and a safe return wherever I traveled. I sincerely thank God that I found the strait gate that led me to Jesus Christ, because I was on the road of destruction. The Holy Spirit guided me in the right direction and I made a decision to submit myself to the Lord, and my life has not been the same. Glory to God! I never understood that I was supposed to receive Jesus as my Lord and Savior and confess my sins, because I was already attending church as a child, reading and hearing the Word of God. I thought those things were a part of accepting Jesus and that was all that mattered.

However, I was wrong, because I never confessed my sins to God until I was twenty-seven years old. I was totally ignorant concerning the difference between accepting Christ, being a Christian, and attending church. The Word of God tells us that people perish because of lack of knowledge, but thank God for Jesus, our sacrificial lamb that gave us eternal life. The Word of God says, "For God so loved the world, that he gave his only begotten Son, that whosoever believeth in him should not perish, but have everlasting life." (John 3:16) The Holy Bible tells us that we have everlasting life because of the love of God. Glory to God!

The book of Romans clearly says, "I beseech you therefore, brethren, by the mercies of God, that ye present your bodies a living sacrifice, holy, acceptable unto God, which is your reasonable service. And be not conformed to this world: but be ye transformed by the renewing of your mind, that ye may prove what is that good, and acceptable, and perfect, will of God." (Romans 12:1–2) These verses let us know that we have responsibilities toward God. We have been given instructions and principles on how to live holy and to renew our minds by studying the Word of God. I believe that we should be obedient and digest this scripture, so that it will take root in our spirit to mature as Christians, while dying to the fleshly things of the world. Amen! Beloved, would you like to drop off some of the former things of the past that have kept you from respecting yourself and God? The kinds of things that lower your self-esteem, which causes you to seek the approval of man and keeps you attached to ungodly things. Hello, somebody!

The remedy is the Holy Spirit, the Spirit of God. He is a teacher, comforter, helper, intercessor, and advocate. We have the opportunity to let the Spirit of God expose our identification to the world as being children of the most high God. The Word of God says, "Now therefore ye are no more strangers and foreigners, but fellow citizens with the saints, and of the household of God;" (Ephesians 2:19). I encourage you to enter in at the strait gate, which will lead you to the road of redemption, and you will not be a stranger in the sight of God. For every soul that is won for the Kingdom of God, the angels in Heaven are praising and worshiping God all day long. Amen! Strait is the gate and narrow is the way, so enter in with faith.

Trust in the Lord

The Word of God distinctly says, "Trust in the *LORD* with all thine heart; and lean not unto thine own understanding. In all thy ways acknowledge him, and he shall direct thy paths." (Proverbs 3:5–6) Beloved, let the truth be told that we need direction. It is good that we are able to rely on our intellect in making decisions, but oftentimes we get advice from others. Why? Because we can't make up our minds and want confirmation on our issues to make decisions. I discovered that there is a voice of authority that we should consider for answers, and that is the Word of God, the Bible. Christians should always search the scriptures for a word from the Lord when confronted with situations. When I am in doubt, I remember Psalm 121:1–2: "I will lift up mine eyes unto the hills, from whence cometh my help. My help cometh from the LORD, which made heaven and earth." I turn to God for an answer and for direction because He is always right. Who have you trusted your dreams, your secrets, and your visions with? In the Bible, there are stories of men and women who trusted God with all their heart and became victorious. God chose people like Moses and Joshua, Deborah and Barak, Elijah and Elisha, John the Baptist, and Apostle Paul, just to name a few. These men and women of God were faced with many challenges when their faith was tested, and God delivered them out of the hand of the enemy because they were on assignment for the Lord!

Beloved, we have to believe that if God delivered great men and women from their perilous situations in biblical times, He can still do the same for us in this age. Your prayers may not be answered in the time frame that you expect, but be patient and have faith that God will do the miraculous in your life. The Word of God declares, "But without faith it is impossible to please him: for he that cometh to God must believe that he is, and that he is a rewarder of them that diligently seek him." (Hebrews 11:6) Amen! The scripture even tells us that we need to believe and have faith, so when are you going to make a decision to receive and believe that you can put your trust in God for all things?

It is amazing how we tend to trust this new wave of technology, which changes daily. Technology is one of the best things that ever happened to humanity. It has ushered in many ways to communicate throughout the world. We communicate by satellite, television, radio, telephone, cell phone, computer, and other electronic devices. These things are good sources of communication and readily available, but are they effective and secure? I encourage everyone to use wisdom and take advantage of these resources, because we need to send and retrieve information on a daily basis, but be careful. There are many things happening daily on this planet, and we need to be informed. I thank God for the various forms of communication because we need to be aware of what is going on in our society, in our nation, and across the world. When we rely on various means of communication, we trust and hope that the information we hear is accurate—especially news about threats to the nation, the economy, the weather, education, transportation, and so forth—so that we can prepare for emergencies and act accordingly. But what happens when a communication device malfunctions; who will be readily available to come to your rescue? Will you get a busy signal on the phone or be asked to wait twenty-four hours, forty-eight hours, seventy-two hours, or even a week for help? What will be your next move when all fails; and whom will you trust?

Nevertheless, when it comes down to trusting in God, many of us waver in our faith, especially when we don't receive the things that we have been praying for. We tend to second-guess whether God will answer our prayers, but whatever happened to being patient and confident? Sometimes we ask God for things and we are not prepared to handle the blessings. I remember the lyrics to a song that said, "God may not come when you want Him, but He is always on time." Do you believe the words to that song? Are you familiar with the words that Jesus said in John 14:13–15? "And whatsoever ye shall ask in my name, that will I do, that the Father may be glorified in the Son. If ye shall ask any thing in my name, I will do it. If ye love me, keep my commandments." If you don't understand what Jesus meant, maybe you can understand this: when you receive your blessings from the Lord, make sure that you thank God for your answered prayers, because Jesus sits on the right hand of the Father making intercession for the saints (see John 17). We need to remember that there is power in the name of Jesus; and there is healing and deliverance in the name of Jesus! God will send someone trustworthy to comfort you with some words of inspiration and wisdom when you are feeling down, sick, or lonely. There are sixty-six books in the Bible, and you can certainly find a word to speak life into your situation. Amen! Many people quote, "Thy word is a lamp unto my feet, and a light unto my path." (Psalm 119:105 NUN) It is a Psalm that reminds Christians that the Word of God is a guide for their lives. I encourage you to take every scripture seriously and try your best to live accordingly. God loves you, so let your light shine that people may see your good works on the earth.

Let God Be Your Decision Maker

Every day we make decisions on various routine things, like deciding what to wear and what to eat, cleaning the house, doing laundry, paying bills, handling relationships, and family and job issues, to name a few. I must say that all of these things are part of our daily lives, but we need to be stress free and take some time to commune with God. I often find that when people need immediate answers, some may toss a coin in the air, roll dice, or call the psychic hotline; and that is their business, but for me and my house, we will seek the Lord! I used to think that the quickest way to get an answer for my situation was to ask someone for advice when I needed support. Sometimes we ask our family, friends, coworkers, or the folks at church for their advice about our situations. I believe that there is nothing wrong with asking people for advice, but you really don't need everybody to know your business, because that leads to gossip. So, if you decide to ask anyone outside of the family for advice, please ask for prayer because "he says" and "she says" become hearsay. You have many options to choose from, but I encourage you to be wise and commune with God on any matter. I believe that it is good to speak to the Holy Spirit, our comforter, when you are in a state of confusion. I talk to the Lord every time I get a quiet moment, because I need direction when I am confused, and strength when I am weak. Glory to God!

Sometimes we need to hear a word from the Lord to let us know whom to trust, because you can't trust everybody. If you ever look at a dollar bill, you will see the words "In God We Trust" written on the back. There was a purpose for the government printing those words on the United States currency. I have discovered that many people don't remember that those words are written on the back, because they are interested only in how much they can get for their bucks! We need to recognize the name of God in the economic field, because some people wanted to have those words removed from the United States currency. It is amazing how people's opinions have such great influence in America. I remember when some people petitioned to ban prayer in schools, and it was accomplished during the 1960s. Although the right to pray was taken out of school, it was not taken out of the heart of the individual. We still have the opportunity to pray and read the Bible at home or other places that are in our comfort zone. Thank God!

I encourage you to read the Word of God, and you will find out about

His characteristics and nature, and your relationship with Him. You will discover that God is present everywhere, and He sees everything that we do. Yes! He knows all things, and you can't hide your sins from God. God is all-powerful, and I know Him to be the source of our strength. Amen! In Psalm 139:1–3, David the king certainly knew about the character of God. He said, "O LORD, thou hast searched me, and known me. Thou knowest my down sitting and mine uprising, thou understandest my thought afar off. Thou compassest my path and my lying down, and art acquainted with all my ways." The Psalm even declares that God sees and knows about us. So whatever you do behind closed doors, away from society, God still knows your secrets. He is an awesome God, and we ought to believe and trust Him for all things. The scripture says, "And we know that all things work together for good to them that love God, to them who are the called according to his purpose." (Romans 8:28) Amen! Have you been called by God? Do you love the Lord? I encourage you to step out on faith and let God show Himself strong and mighty in your life to expose your gifts and talents to the world.

In the Old Testament God's servant Moses was appointed to lead the children of Israel out of the land of Egypt, after they had been in captivity for four hundred years. It was only after the tenth plague that Pharaoh decided to let them leave to worship God. The story tells us that as they began to cross the Red Sea, Pharaoh had a change in mind and went after the children of Israel with his army. The people feared that they were going to be killed by the Egyptians, but God had another plan for their lives. Beloved, there will come a time in your life when you will experience the feeling of fear, but I've experienced that fear is a feeling that does not last very long. It is usually replaced with the feeling of relief, joy, or happiness after the situation is resolved. Moses had faith that God was going to fight their battle. The Bible says, "And Moses said unto the people, Fear ye not, stand still, and see the salvation of the LORD, which he will shew to you to day: for the Egyptians whom ye have seen to day, ye shall see them again no more for ever. The LORD shall fight for you, and ye shall hold your peace." (Exodus 14:13–14) Moses believed that God would rescue them from the hand of the enemy, but the children of Israel did not believe until they were safe on dry land. They praised God and began to dance and shout for their deliverance from bondage. Beloved, when we are delivered from our enemies, we ought to give God the glory and honor that is due His name, because He loves us and His mercies endure forever. Amen!

We need to recognize when the favor of God is upon our life and not be overwhelmed by the feeling of fear. I pray for your health and strength in the Lord, that you will develop confidence and faith in God. The Word of God says, "For God hath not given us the spirit of fear; but of power, and of love, and of a sound mind." (2 Timothy 1:7) I encourage you to praise God when you are going through situations, and you will come out with a victorious testimony.

Part Four
More Than a Conqueror

Military Spirit
(Dedicated to young adults)

Many of us have a military spirit like Joshua, Moses' successor. God told Joshua to lead the children of Israel into the Promised Land, the land of milk and honey, in order to receive their inheritance, but they had to conquer the land to possess the territory. What do I mean by a military spirit? A spirit of combat, an attitude of rebellion against the enemy, and you are ready to fight back by any means necessary. Some of us are always ready to fight back, especially when we are angry or when we have to stand up for what is right and take action. However, we need to learn whether we are being disciplined or threatened.

I have experienced that when you are being disciplined, you receive some kind of correction for your punishment or you are being trained for something. On the other hand, when you are threatened the intent is to harm you in any form or fashion. Hello, somebody! I've learned that God will discipline us so that we can function adequately in this world because He loves us. Whereas Satan, who is the Christian's enemy, intends to harm you and to keep you in fear, so it will be easy for him to defeat you. However, Jesus said, "The thief cometh not, but for to steal, and to kill, and to destroy: I am come that they might have life, and that they might have it more abundantly." (John 10:10) I believe the word of the Lord and choose to have an abundant life and be discipline by God anytime—especially when I need to be corrected for wrongdoing.

The Bible tells us that God had a great assignment for Joshua, and he obeyed the instructions without hesitation. Do you follow instructions? If you are still learning, just keep reading and find out what happened to Joshua and the children of Israel. Joshua was told to conquer the territory and possess the land, but there was a great wall in the way. It was the walls of the city of Jericho. He was instructed to march around the walls of Jericho for six days, but on the seventh day, to march seven times. There was preparation for the assignment, and a host of faithful people were chosen for the task. Joshua was instructed to appoint seven priests to bear before the Ark, seven trumpets of rams' horns, and armed men to fight. The Ark was the dwelling place of God, and only the priest was able to carry that piece of furniture. The priest marched with the army and carried no weapons, because God's presence was with them.

Joshua was instructed to command the people not to shout or make any noise, until the last march. It seemed like a lot of marching, but the walls were in the way. Hello, somebody! Joshua and the children of Israel marched around the city of Jericho for six days, and on the seventh day they marched seven times. The priests blew their trumpets. The people shouted unto the Lord with a great shout, and the walls of Jericho came falling down. Amen!

Beloved, if there are any walls or obstacles standing in your way, it is time to tear them down and to move forward to get your possessions. Glory to God! You have to envision the victory in your mind and be confident that you are more than a conqueror. We have to remember that for every trial, every mountain, and every valley that we encounter, God will take us through. We have to believe that we shall pursue and recover all that we had lost. Glory to God! We have to endure patiently and stop being in a rush to have everything in an instant. Sometimes you have to wait for the manifestation of what is revealed to you in dreams and visions. Amen! We have to learn to become obedient and follow instructions like Joshua. We were born with a purpose, and there is greatness inside of us waiting to be revealed. We can become doctors, lawyers, teachers, scientists, or disciples for Christ, just to name a few. I encourage you to pray and believe that you will finish what you have started and you will have the victory!

Obedient Soldiers for the Lord

Beloved, I believe that we need to be ready to combat the evil forces that have increased its activity in the world. We need to purpose in our minds to become Christian soldiers for the Lord and to stop fighting against our brothers and sisters. Hello, somebody! We are living in some trying times, and people need to know that Jesus loves them and there is salvation through Jesus Christ. Many things are happening in the world with a ripple effect: hurricanes, typhoons, fires, earthquakes, floods in diverse places, and the list can go on and on. We have been warned in the Bible that these things are going to occur. God has been sending out His messengers for centuries, and the majority of people have yet to believe that Christ is soon to return. John the Baptist was sent as a forerunner of Christ, and he preached the baptism of repentance for the remission of sins. The Lord sent him on a mission to tell the people to repent, for the Kingdom of Heaven was at hand. He baptized men, women, and children. John the Baptist witnessed and warned the people with the voice of authority. "John answered, saying unto them all, I indeed baptize you with water; but one mightier than I cometh, the latchet of whose shoes I am not worthy to unloose: he shall baptize you with the Holy Ghost and with fire." (Luke 3:16) He had to let the people know that Jesus was on the way.

We are living in the Millennium, and I can assure you that Jesus is on the way. I encourage you to study the Word of God and get to know Jesus for yourself, so that you won't be deceived by anyone pretending to be Christ. In the Word of God, Jesus warned us about those who would come claiming to be the Christ. In Matthew 24:5–6, Jesus said, "For many shall come in my name, saying, I am Christ; and shall deceive many. And ye shall hear of wars and rumors of wars: see that ye be not troubled: for all these things must come to pass, but the end is not yet." Beloved, we have an opportunity to receive Jesus into our hearts as our Lord and Savior. There should be no delay in trying to figure out whom you should serve, because the hour has come and God is looking for the true worshippers who will worship Him in spirit and in truth. Amen!

We have the opportunity to receive Jesus as Lord, and the invitation is written in the Bible. In Romans 10:9–10, the Word of God says, "That if thou shalt confess with thy mouth the Lord Jesus, and shalt believe in thine heart that God hath raised him from the dead, thou shalt be saved. For with the heart man believeth unto righteousness; and with the mouth confession is made unto salvation." I love the Lord, and my heart desires that those who have not accepted Jesus into their hearts will strongly consider the invitation. I believe that some of us can use a change in our lifestyles, especially if we have been running away from the truth about ourselves. It's time to stop living in a world of deception that can lead you to believe everything that you hear. It is important to read interesting books to gain knowledge, but we should read the Bible to find out about the power of God. The Word of God says, "That your faith should not stand in the wisdom of men, but in the power of God." (1 Corinthians 2:5) We ought to give up and forsake the desirable things of the world that cause us to sin, because it is the lust of the eyes, the lust of the flesh, and the pride of life that lead us into temptation.

When we commit ourselves to the Lord Jesus, we are converted from our old nature and we take on the nature of Christ. When we receive Christ, we are saved by His grace because of Jesus's death, burial, and resurrection. Glory to God! Are you ready to become a Christian solider for the army of the Lord? You don't have to wear a new outfit to accept Christ into your life. God will accept you in any state of mind or condition, and He will forgive you for your sins. I was not the best kid on the block or the cleanest person in the world before I repented my sins. In fact, I was drowning in my sinful state, but God had another plan for me when I accepted Jesus as my personal Savior. I extend the invitation to you to accept Christ into your hearts. Wherever you are or whatever you might be doing at this very moment, don't be ashamed to be a sanctified witness for the Lord, because if God cleaned me up, I know that He can do the same for you. I pray that God will bless you always and keep you in perfect peace!

Take God at His Word

There is always a word from the Lord of edification, exhortation, and comfort to those who are in need. Many people don't take the Word of God seriously, even when He tells His servants to deliver a message. One day I received a message from the Lord about the gifts of the Holy Spirit and how God was going to use me as a vessel in the ministry of deliverance. I mourned and groaned from the depths of my soul because of the task that God had commissioned me to do. Most of the tasks that we are instructed to do affect our emotions. However, I found out that God will sustain us and strengthen us for the task of helping those in need. When we witness the miraculous healings and deliverance of God's people, it is done for the glory of God to be manifested on the earth, so that all who never believed in God will witness His mighty power.

It is not easy for me to warn people concerning things the Holy Spirit reveals to me, but I must obey God as a disciple of Christ, even though some people ignore the warnings. The disciples were chosen vessels commissioned by Jesus to continue the work that He began to do throughout the world. Some of the work included saving lost souls, healing, teaching, baptizing, and turning the hearts of the people back to God. If you are a Christian, you should purpose in your heart to pick up your cross and follow Jesus as He told His disciples to do. I believe that God will prepare us for the work of the ministry to edify the body of Christ. We will not bear the cross alone, because the Holy Spirit will teach us whatever we need to know. I thank God that some people have been appointed as apostles, prophets, evangelists, pastors, and teachers to labor for the Kingdom of God. Whatever we do, it should be done for the glory of God and not to glorify ourselves. It is easy to become puffed up thinking that we are the only anointed saints of God. We have to remember that God will use anyone that He chooses. I found out that some ushers, musicians, missionaries, deacons, and laypeople in the church have been appointed and anointed to labor for the Kingdom of God as well. When we come together as one in the body of Christ, we can reach a multitude of souls, like the apostles did in the book of Acts. Amen! Together we can destroy the works of Satan operating in the lives of our brothers and sisters who are bound and want to be set free.

The word of the Lord spoken in Isaiah 55:11 says, "So shall my word be that goeth forth out of my mouth: it shall not return unto me void, but it shall accomplish that which I please, and it shall prosper in the thing whereto I sent it." We ought to become more confident in what we are reading in the Bible and stop wavering in our faith, because the Word of God is the sword of the Spirit. Beloved, we need to start quoting scriptures from the Bible that give us confidence and strength. Psalm 27:1 says, "The *LORD* is my light and my salvation; whom shall I fear? the *LORD* is the strength of my life; of whom shall I be afraid?" It is good to memorize scriptures, because there will be times when you will need to quote scripture to encourage yourself during your dark and dreary days. You may not remember the entire scripture, but a verse may even be sufficient for your situation, such as Psalm 23:4: "Yea, though I walk through the valley of the shadow of death, I will fear no evil: for thou art with me; thy rod and thy staff they comfort me." There are so many scriptures in the Bible that we can glean from to help us increase our faith. What are you waiting for? Study the Word of God and equip yourself for the work of the ministry, because the harvest is plentiful.

Faith in God

Prayer is the key, and faith unlocks the door! I had to witness to myself and develop great faith when there was no one around. In 1985, I laid in a hospital bed for about one month and seven days on antibiotics because of an infection in my left foot. I know that it was by faith and the grace of God that I did not lose my foot. Glory to God! Everyone that came to visit me, whether it was family, friends, or the doctors, always had a sad look on their faces because my foot was black as tar, and there was no hope. It is amazing how people that you are connected with can feel what you are going through because of their compassion. The floor that I was on had patients with some of their limbs amputated, but I was determined to leave the hospital with both feet, because I trusted God. I believed that I was going to be healed in the name of Jesus. I remember my oldest brother had given me his Bible, and I kept it in my bed for thirty-seven days. During those days I had some great conversations with God. One day while I was praying to the Lord, I began pouring out my heart, saying things like, "I don't want to lose my foot, because I'm not married yet. I don't have children and I want to go back to school; I need something to do because my dance career is over." I cried out, "Lord, please don't let me lose my foot; I'm going to trust you to help me." In reality, I was really frightened about being in the hospital and not being able to help myself.

I learned a great lesson on being thankful for my life while suffering on my sickbed. I thought about my lifestyle and the progress that I was making in the performing arts. I had no regrets about the sacrifices that I had made in spending money on dance lessons and acting classes, because I enjoyed performing. My foot condition certainly changed my way of thinking, and I found out that fun doesn't last forever. I had plenty of time to think about how I was going to start over after I leave the hospital. I kept thinking about my past experiences and how I used to have fun running to the club and running in and out of the church. I was trying to be a good person by attending church on Sundays and satisfying my flesh by hanging out at the disco four times a week. I began to feel guilty lying in that hospital bed, because I spent more time at the disco and less time in the church. I was disappointed with myself, because I had stopped giving God the glory for the gifts and talents that I was born with. I had to pray to keep my sanity, because I was not able to walk and my foot kept draining from the inflammation. In fact, being in that condition made me learn how to stop being selfish. I asked God to forgive me, and He had mercy on me. I called a prayer warrior who was a friend of my family to pray for me, and she made an effort to visit. I know that God sent her, because she said some things to me that revived my spirit. I thanked God for everybody who was praying for me, because I gained a lot of confidence and faith in God while I was on the road to recovery. I left the hospital healed in the name of Jesus, and I could not wait to tell people about God answering my prayers. Amen! The Lord started blessing me with many of the things that I asked for, and I started attending church more frequently that same year.

However, the next year, 1986, I started slowing down my witnessing about Jesus. I felt like the Lord was satisfied with me, and I started performing again and hanging out in the theater club. I was slipping back into my old ways, and the people that I hung around with were not saved (no relationship with Christ). I was not strong enough in the Word of God or disciplined well enough to keep my distance from the theater parties. I had to ask myself, *What was all of that stuff about telling God that I was going to do this and that, while I was on my sickbed?* Well, I found out that when we are afraid something devastating is going to happen to us, we tend to plead our case with God, hoping that He will have mercy on us instantly. Have you ever been through a devastating situation in your life? Little did I know that God already knew that I was not going to be obedient for long. In fact, one day I had a bad experience that made me think twice about submitting to the will of the Lord again.

I was returning from the bank with my job's petty cash, and as soon as I walked in front of my employer's door, two young men robbed me. It was very strange, and everything around me became silent. I was not afraid, because I remembered hearing in my conscience a voice saying to be careful. I thought my mind was playing tricks on me that day. I ignored my conscience and wanted to see what really was going to happen to me, since other people were walking down the block. I was really in for a surprise when two guys started walking behind me. One fellow held me in a choke hold, while the other stepped on my foot and took the envelope of money out of my bag. I thought that I was dreaming, and the only thing that I could say was, "Lord, please don't let him cut my throat." Then I passed out. When I woke up, I found myself sitting on the ground. It was the weirdest experience that I ever encountered. I was in such a state of shock and was not able to cry. I knew that I was a target that day because I was wearing a long ankle skirt and an orthopedic shoe on my left foot. There was no way that I could have run down the street, because the incident happened in front of my employer's place of business.

I know for sure that God was with me during that entire experience. I even realized that the small voice I heard on that day was the Holy Spirit warning me to be careful, but my stubbornness got me into trouble. I had to explain the story concerning the incident to the policemen that afternoon. I never mentioned that I heard the voice of God warning me to be careful, because I assumed that they would have thought I was crazy. In fact, so many things were going on in my mind, I even felt like I turned my back on God by not letting the policemen know that God had saved my life. I thought that if I shared that story about hearing a voice, they would have taken me to the Bellevue Hospital psychiatric center, because it was only a few blocks away. After that incident, I never went back to the bank alone. My foot condition eventually became better after a few months. I was considering going back on the stage because I was bored, and my drama never stopped.

Drama! Drama! Drama! I started hanging out again the next year, but in a more quiet setting. In 1987 things seem different with me. I started having heavenly visions and discerning things I never thought were possible. One morning after I left the after-hours club, I met my mother at church for the 7:30 AM service. That particular morning the Spirit of God came over me, and I went down to the altar and received Jesus as my personal Savior. Amen! Many great things started happening to me, and I was maturing. I started attending church and reading the Bible again. I even landed a new job and enrolled into college.

I knew that the best was yet to come and I ventured on to a number of things over the years. I raised my nephew and ministered to people about God's grace and mercy. I read the Bible as if it were a regular textbook, because I was trying to get to know about Jesus. I tried to understand what God was trying to tell me about the stories in the Bible and the blessings that I was receiving, but I could not comprehend. I felt like I was in a tug-of-war and was being attacked by the enemy from all sides, but God was fighting my battles. I didn't know about putting on the full armor of God. I was not aware that the sword of the spirit, which is the Word of God, taught me how to pull down the strongholds in my life. I read the Bible because I wanted to be educated. I was thirsting for knowledge and wanted a closer relationship with God. I read the

Word of God over and over, until I began to get revelations on things concerning the heart of humanity. I began searching for answers, and God began to open doors for me to share my experiences with other Christians. I've learned that some experiences can leave you in such a positive state of mind that you'll never want to turn away from God and repeat the same mistakes anymore! When you are moving forward and growing in the Lord, try to surround yourself with people who are going in the same direction, so you won't go off track and waver in your faith. I really believe that prayer is the key and faith unlocks the door! Which would you choose to flow in your life, faith or fear?

Preparation for Kingdom Work

When you are chosen to do the will of God, He will prepare you for the task and equip you to be able to stand against the fiery darts of the enemy. Yes, we will encounter some experiences dealing with warfare, but I found out that God will fight our battle. I kept running away from the task that God wanted me to do and tried to stay in secular school. I was not able to pay for classes to continue my education and was encountering all types of negative situations. However, one day the Holy Spirit stopped me in my tracks after I finished graduate school and ordered my footsteps to Bible school and seminary. I was on the road to new beginnings and said, "Yes to your will, Lord. I will win souls for You, and the Gospel of Jesus will be preached throughout the world."

Submitting my will to the Lord was the best thing that ever happened to me. I confessed that I would be obedient and become serious about studying the Bible, because we can't use our natural instincts to defeat the enemy. It is not a physical war that is occurring, but a spiritual battle. Christians should be aware that we have been given authority on the earth to defend ourselves against all wicked works. Jesus said to His disciples, "Behold, I give unto you power to tread on serpents and scorpions, and over all the power of the enemy: and nothing shall by any means hurt you." (Luke 10:19) If you are a child of God, you are entitled to the same power that was given to Jesus's disciples. I believe that there is power in the name of Jesus. When you receive the Holy Spirit, you will be empowered with the gifts of the Spirit. Some of the gifts are prophecy, speaking in tongues (other languages), and interpreting tongues. There are also the gift of healing, the gift of faith, and the working of miracles.

You will also be empowered with the word of knowledge, word of wisdom, and discerning of spirits. Even though the saints of God can be blessed with these gifts, it is more important that our names are written in Heaven. Amen! I thank God that Jesus ascended into Heaven and gave some gifts to the church, so that the saints of God will continue the work Jesus accomplished during His earthly ministry. The Bible says, "And he gave some, apostles; and some, prophets; and some, evangelists; and some, pastors and teachers; For the perfecting of the saints for the work of the ministry, for the edifying of the body of Christ:" (Ephesians 4:11–12). Praise the Lord! There is plenty of work in the mission field, and a lot of people are in need of godly counseling.

Have you accepted your assignment from the Potter (God)? Are you laboring for the Kingdom of God yet? Jesus made it clear in His teachings that "My sheep hear my voice, and I know them, and they follow me:" (John 10:27). Hello, somebody! I believe that every Christian is responsible for winning souls for the Kingdom of God, and we don't need a specific function in the church to prove our qualifications, because it is the anointing that destroys the yoke. Amen! It is important that you study the Word of God for yourself and ask the Holy Spirit to help you understand the scriptures. If you ever become discouraged because you are not a minister in the church, remember that you can preach the Gospel of Jesus Christ under the leading of the Holy Spirit anytime. Most of all, please make sure that your family receives Jesus into their hearts, so that you will see them again in Heaven!

Lord, Shape Me and Mold Me

My walk with Christ didn't just happen in the latter years of my life; it started during the early years when I was taken to church for a naming ceremony, considered to be a christening service. The pastor sprinkled water on my head and offered me unto the Lord to be blessed and to receive godparents as my second parents. The godparents had to take an oath that they would help raise me and take on the responsibility of taking care of me, if my parents were no longer able. At least, that was the commission of the godparents according to the ordinance of the church. Christening services are not always conducted in the same manner, depending on the church denomination. However, it was the responsibility of my parents to make sure that I learned about Jesus. My mother and grandmother taught us how to read the Bible and pray. We were taught a prayer for blessing our food, a prayer for going to sleep, and a prayer for getting up in the morning. We attended church services on Sundays. The adults attended the morning preaching service, while the children attended Sunday school. Many of the things that we learned about God were intended as the groundwork for us to be prepared to become workers for Christ. It was always praise, prayer, and everyone coming in one accord at church or at home when we were young. When we became older, however, things began to change and a few of us decided to do other things on Sundays. My mother and grandmother were not happy about the lifestyles of some of us, but peer pressure was part of the problem. I believe that things would have been different in our lives if my father had been present to help raise our family. My mother gave birth to eight children—four boys and four girls. I was the sixth child out of the eight, and we had fun despite the confusion and warfare surrounding us!

Warfare

The warfare that we encounter today can not be compared with the warfare that occurred in the lives of men and women in the Bible. Everyone that God appointed to intercede on behalf of the children of Israel had great faith and believed that God was on his or her side—men and women like Elijah the prophet, Ruth, Esther, King Solomon, Daniel the prophet, Paul the apostle, and the disciples. The few that I named were confident that God would show Himself strong and mighty in the midst of their perils because they were chosen to do specific tasks. The apostle Paul wrote in 2 Timothy 3:12–13, "Yea, and all that will live godly in Christ Jesus shall suffer persecution. But evil men and seducers shall wax worse and worse, deceiving, and being deceived." Every Christian laboring for the Kingdom of God should be aware that he or she will encounter opposition at some point, because the enemy hates to see people delivered from his bondage. We have to remember that Satan targets children at a young age because he suspects that God has ordained them to witness the Gospel of Jesus.

I remember my father living with us for a few years while I was young. I used to see his army suit hanging in the closet and the postal uniform that he wore to work. I looked forward to his coming home, but

I was always asleep by the time he arrived. We assumed that our parents were enjoying their lives together and were happily married—at least that is what we witnessed. I'm sure that they shared some great days together. However, there was a lot of drama going on in our household with favoritism toward my sisters and brothers. My older siblings wanted to be in charge when my mother was not at home, but no one ever paid them any attention. We never knew that our parents were having problems, because they never argued in front of us. I guess all of my parents' disagreements happened behind closed doors. I don't remember how long my father lived with us, but he certainly wasn't around on the day that I ate a half bottle of baby aspirin. This was one of my mother's worst nightmares. The aspirin tasted like cherry candy, and I gave some to one of my younger brothers. We became sick, and I almost passed out. I was taken to the hospital and had to get my stomach pumped because I had taken an overdose of the aspirin. That experience taught me the difference between cherry candy and cherry baby aspirin. I am grateful that God had another plan for me to live and not die to declare the glory of the Lord.

There was always something going on in our household, and my mother was always at the emergency room with one of her eight children. It was not easy for her to manage us after my father permanently left, but I thank God that my grandmother moved in to help us. I believe that it was painful for my mother, but we were young and didn't understand anything about separation. My family was taught to love one another, and there was no hatred in my heart for the absence of my dada. My father used to visit us after we became older, but that was not good enough for my brothers, because they needed nurturing from a man. It was definitely a struggle, because my brothers were never taught to be responsible by the voice of a man. The voice of authority came from my mother and grandmother's teaching. Whenever we got out of line, the belt was the form of discipline to change our behavior.

However, the warfare during my childhood continued to go on, and I was back in the emergency room again. I had fallen over a wooden milk crate that had metal stripping, and it cut off the tip of my tongue. The doctors had to do some serious stitching to my tongue, which was not a very comfortable feeling. I was not able to eat anything for a while, except for liquids and ice cream. This incident was another attack from the devil to prevent me from speaking the Word of God in the future, and I am convinced that I was raised up for such a time as this to do the will of God. I never experienced being nurtured or disciplined by my father, but I purposed in my heart to get to know our Heavenly Father. I discovered that God gives you another kind of nurturing that is unexplainable. I understand now why my grandmother always said, "You better listen to God, because He will take care of you." My grandmother was certainly right about what God will do, because He has kept and protected me throughout the years. It would have been a good experience to give my father paper ties and cards on Father's Day, but there was always Mother's Day to make a card for my mom.

My mother knew that the enemy was after her children, because we were always in some type of trouble, and she became accustomed to singing, praying, and calling on the name of Jesus. There were all types of demonic influences in our neighborhood. I remember some of our neighbors used to deal with witchcraft and sorcery. They held tarot card readings and carried wishbones and stuffed rabbits' feet. It seemed like Satan was outside waiting for us to mess up, so that he could turn us away from the love of God, but the devil is a liar. My grandmother and the other mothers in our family used to assemble and wage war (strategic prayer) in the spirit for all the children. Praise the Lord! The enemy will use devices and people to carry out his plan of destruction on the elect of God, but I thank God that somebody prayed for our family. I pray that you will draw near to God and experience the great love that He has for you. We are God's special children, and we are fearfully and wonderfully made in the image of God.

God loves you and He will never leave or forsake you, regardless of the tribulations you may encounter. I encountered a lot of warfare growing up, and I know that I am not the only person in the world who has had mishaps. I remember following my sister and her friends to the store once, and somehow I could not keep up with them and I got lost. I was wandering around the neighborhood for a long time trying to find my way back home. I was stopped by a woman who was giving out tracts about Jesus. She knew that I was lost after I told her my story, and she tried to kidnap me. I was lucky that my cousin saw us standing together and ran over to see what was going on. The woman claimed that I was her daughter, but she could not prove our relationship, and the police had to get involved to resolve the matter. I thank God that my cousin happened to come in the area where I was lost, because that woman had other intentions for me. I certainly had a lot of drama going on in my life when I was a child. I was like a sheep gone astray, and God led my cousin's footsteps on that day. Praise the Lord!

I always knew that something evil was after me, because a demonic spirit would show up in my dreams and God would always come to my rescue. I believe that God was using me in my dreams to help my friends get out of trouble. There was always something evil chasing us in the dream, but I knew how to escape my dreams. Yes! I knew that I was in a dream and at some point, I was going to wake up in reality. I was confident that my dream strategies were going to work. I know that I was a strange child, but I had a lot of wisdom and was able to end my dreams. I also knew that God had something to do with rescuing me from the snares of the enemy. I believe that God was training me in spiritual warfare during my early years to prepare me for the future. Praise the Lord! I know that my experiences sound bizarre, but some unusual things used to happen to me, and I began to write about my dream experiences.

In fact, I was a sleepwalker for a while, and I never understood sleepwalking experiences. My sister told me that I used to get up in the middle of the night and do strange things. Maybe I needed some help as a child and no one ever considered the thought, but thank God that I live a more balanced life today. People might say that I had a vivid imagination, but stuff happens. I am sure there are other people with some interesting stories that will leave you in frenzy, and they may be afraid to share their stories. Let me clarify that I did not experience bad dreams every night throughout my life; they only occurred occasionally. I write about my experiences because there is some kind of connection between the natural and supernatural worlds. If you believe that there are angels, then you are likely to believe that there are demons also. In the New Testament you will find biblical stories that address the presence of angels and demons. In the book of Luke, the angel Gabriel was sent by God to Mary with a message. The Bible says, "And the angel said unto her, Fear not, Mary: for thou hast found favour with God. And behold, thou shalt conceive in thy womb, and bring forth a son, and shalt call his name *JESUS*." (Luke 1:30–31) Jesus was a prime target of the devil, especially after He was baptized by John the Baptist and God announced him as being His Son. In Matthew 4:1–3, the Word of God says, "Then was Jesus led up of the Spirit into the wilderness to be tempted of the devil. And when he had fasted forty days and forty nights, he was afterward a hungered. And when the tempter came to him, he said, If thou be the Son of God, command that these stones be made bread." Even though Jesus was tempted by the devil, He knew His authoritative position on the earth because He was the Son of God. Jesus did not obey the devil's commands, because He really had power over the devil. The apostle Paul said, "For we wrestle not against flesh and blood, but against principalities, against powers, against the rulers of the darkness of this world, against spiritual wickedness in high places." (Ephesians 6:12) There are other accounts in the Bible that mention the presence of demonic activity, but my purpose is to show you where an example can be found in the scriptures.

We seem to be surrounded by the presence of good and evil, because there is always some type of supernatural activity happening around the world, but there will come a time when Satan will no longer corrupt the world. I had no knowledge of spiritual warfare until I was in my thirties, and I was curious to find out. I began reading stories in the Bible about spiritual warfare and how God fights our battles. If you read the New Testament books of the Bible, you will see that the apostle Paul and the other apostles encountered a lot of warfare from negative forces. I have come to the realization that God will send a host of angels to ward off the negative forces in the spirit realm, which you are not able to see with the natural eye. The Holy Spirit was really helping me to understand supernatural occurrences, because I had an encounter with some African spirits in the 1970s. Yes! Three African warriors, tall and slim with white tribal marks on their faces and carrying spears, were standing at the side of my bed. I was not certain at the time whether I had experienced a dream or a vision that night. One of the men was holding my head and chanting with a spear in his hand. The second warrior was standing at my feet chanting with a spear, while the third warrior painted a white line on my face and body. I was crying and unable to move. It was the scariest thing that ever happened to me. I woke up that night in a cold sweat, checking my body for the white marks and finding none, and then I realized that it was only a dream. I told my family about the experience that morning, and they laughed because they thought that I had seen a movie and had a bad dream about what I had seen on television. There was no African movie being shown on the night of my dream. That experience taught me that some people ignore things that just might be more important to others.

However, that was not the end of the African spirits. I had another encounter with the same tribe thirty years later on a specific date: June 21, 2006. I woke up from a nap and saw a colorful tribal mask in the ceiling. I had to look up twice to see if what I saw was real, but it faded away. I knew that it was a sign and a warning for me to be careful. Beloved, that was only the beginning of the mask, because on June 23, 2006, I received a tribal mask in the mail. One of my friends had traveled to Africa and brought back some gifts. I was excited about the gift because it brought some closure to my teenage experience with the African warriors who painted my body in the dream. I also shared the story with my mother, and she was surprised as well. My friend told me that the mask was from the Masai tribe in Africa. I was anxious to share the story concerning this mask with some other people, and I was informed that it was a ceremonial mask. It was suggested to me that I should take the mask out of my house, because it was considered a deity that people worshipped. I knew that something was strange about the mask, because I had water problems for three days in my kitchen and bathroom. I really wanted to keep the mask, but eventually I took it out of my house, and the water problems stopped. I am not trying to make this story sound spooky, but the mask experiences did not stop completely!

In the summer of 2008, I was coming out of the train station and a woman was handing out flyers for a movie that was going to be shown that night. Lo and behold, the name of the movie was *Masai: The Rain Warriors*. Well! I understood why I had water problems for three days while the mask was in my house. I believe that the spirit of the Masai tribe was following me for a long time. I wonder if it was a sign to let me know that my family roots were from the Masai tribe, but I will never know unless I research my family history back to the tribes of Africa. The only African connection I could think of was my ex-husband, but he was from a different tribe.

In life we experience all kinds of things to prepare us for the future, and I believe that God was preparing me to become a prayer warrior (an intercessor) for this present time. As a child, I trusted God to help me, and I trust Him even more as an adult because my warfare is on a greater level. I am convinced that God will empower and equip you with the gifts of the Spirit to be effective Christian soldiers for the Kingdom of God. Amen!

Part Five
Deliver Me from Myself

Desires of the Heart

At some point in life everyone wants to fulfill a desire that they long to pursue to satisfy their need. I have discovered that when you are gifted with many talents, it becomes hard to decide which you should try first. I was fortunate to have the abilities to draw, sew, dance, write, and act (in performances). God blessed me with these gifts so that I can help others, as well as myself, to fulfill desires. I was so impressed with the entertainment world and wanted to try acting, singing, dancing, and modeling. Whatever the entertainment business had to offer, I wanted to experience it. I took acting classes and dance lessons to prepare myself for the stage. I even posed for a photography school to get free pictures for my portfolio. I worked two jobs to pay for my lessons, but that was the sacrifice I had to make to fulfill my dreams. I performed for several years in off-Broadway plays that many people never knew existed, but that was show business.

However, in life you can become whatever your heart desires, but whatever career that you consider, it's important to research and get advice to avoid careless mistakes. When you are living at home with your parents, you tend to become comfortable with being dependent, and you don't see the reality of paying bills. I wasted a lot of time having fun and chasing my dreams of being an entertainer after I graduated from high school. I discovered that I was not able to keep up with the nightlife. There were too many parties and the casting couch, and that was one piece of furniture I did not want to experience. I realized that I had to slow down and regroup, because I wasn't making any money in the theater world. It was time for me to become more serious about my life. I was tired of having boyfriend after boyfriend, and looking into so many faces didn't make sense to me anymore. I felt like it was time for me to have a husband and become devoted to one man. Hello, somebody! I made a commitment not to leave my mother's house until I was married, and when I got the engagement ring, I wasted no time saying, "I do!"

Married but Not in Love

Lies, lies, lies! We really need to start telling the truth about our relationships, because many of us get married for the wrong reasons. I was certainly in the category of liar's, until it was time for me to split the scene. I never made it to the part of the marriage to experience "till death do we part." The only thing that became dead was the infatuation. I am guilty of closing my eyes when I said, "I do." I even forgot to open the Bible to find the scriptures pertaining to husbands and wives. I confess to having a spirit of rebellion toward the Word of God, and that will never happen again. I found out that God is not playing with us, and we really need to get it right when it comes down to marriage and commitment. It is a shame, and there is no excuse for some people refusing to be doers of the Word of God—and I confess to the charge of not being a doer. God knew that my spouse and I were living a lie. I guess you can call us hypocrites, because we are adults and should have known better. The Word of God specifically says, "Wives, submit yourselves unto your own husbands, as it is fit in the Lord. Husbands, love your wives, and be not bitter against them." (Colossians 3:18–19) We prayed together on our knees at night and we attended church, but we neglected to study the Bible together. My marriage was more like two people living together trying to find out whether they could stay together. We tried to be in accord in many things that we shared, even though we came from different backgrounds. The compromising of our lifestyles lasted only a few years, but as I said before, people get married for the wrong reasons. I lived in the suburbs and commuted at least six days a week because my family, job, school, church, and the students I tutored were in the city. I had to visit my mother at least twice a week to check on her. My spouse was well aware that I was a multitasking person before we got married, and I came with a package full of drama! Beloved, one of the reasons that I'm sharing this story is to make you aware of the reality of getting married for the wrong reasons. The years that I spent with my spouse were quite interesting, and we shared some great moments.

I learned that when two people agree to be together, they have to be strong to endure the consequences of sleeping alone some nights. You have to endure the fact that you are not really in love, but have strong feelings toward one another. However, when you discover that your marriage is not working out, it is good to get some counseling. If that does not work out, then someone needs to have the courage to say, "I think that we should separate." It took a lot of courage for us to come to that agreement. In fact, I was interested in making sure that I got half of the money that we had saved in the bank for a rainy day, because that was fair and equitable. Lo and behold, the time came when the relationship was becoming sort of rocky. I knew that it was time for me to vacate the premises, because strange things started happening in our apartment. We started hearing noises at night coming from the roof. It sounded like children running across the floor playing in the attic. We found out that baby raccoons were living in the attic for a few weeks, and eventually the apartment management had them removed. The drama in the house did not stop. After the raccoons left, bees (insects) started showing up dead on the floor in our bedroom and bathroom. I knew that it was time for me to move out. It was interesting that I never saw any dead bees on my side of the room. They seemed to die on the other side of the bed near the window. I tried to seal up the air conditioner, because we thought they were coming in through a hole, but that was not the case. We found out that there was a crack in the wall outside of the building on the first floor and the bees had made a honeycomb. This was the last sign that I needed to confirm that it was time to leave ASAP (as soon as possible). The lease was up for the year, and we had no intentions to renew it. Things seemed to be moving in a timely fashion, and most of my bags were already packed. I knew that God was preparing me for some critical moments in my life, and I was not leaving with any animosity in my heart. I believe that when you are separating, it is good to leave on a positive note to avoid going to court.

Only God knew what was really going on in my household, and I need not say any more! I moved back into the city and had a new beginning. God had something greater in store for me. I was still in school trying to finish a degree program and looking for a job at the same time. In 1998 God blessed me with a new job, and two weeks later I found an apartment in a co-op dwelling. I love the Lord. He always looks out for me even when I don't deserve it. God is my provider and my strength, and I will always give Him the honor and praise that is due His name. I was so fortunate that my spouse agreed to help me move into my new apartment. Praise the Lord! I really was happy about moving back into the city from Long Island, because my commute had been about one and a half hours. I also regret getting married for the wrong reasons, and I certainly learned some lessons that I don't want to repeat. The marriage experience made me strong and wise. That experience taught me to make sure that God is in the center of any relationship that I pursue in the future. In fact, if the question of marriage ever comes up again, I'll have to fast and pray for months to get an answer from the Lord!

Separated but Not Divorced

I am convinced that my health and strength come from the Lord, because He kept me in line and made sure that I did not lose my mind after my separation. Yes! I continued to attend church, but I started hanging out in the clubs again because I was bored. I had one foot on the dance floor and the other foot on the church floor. It was time for me to make a decision about what my greatest desire was, and since I was not sure, God led me in the right direction. Living alone for the first time was certainly a rude awakening. I kept myself busy to avoid thinking about being lonely. I started tutoring at the library literacy center twice a week after work. I also took tennis and driving lessons to keep me busy on Saturdays. I had something to do every day of the week, because I needed to be motivated and not depressed. I became overwhelmed with all of my activities and had very little time to cook and clean my house, so I got some help from my family. I must admit that getting help was the best thing for me, because I was thirty-eight years old, living alone, and trying to figure out if I wanted to be separated and have a boyfriend. I had some interesting conversations with my girlfriends, and as a result, I decided that it was time for me to have a companion. It was a big mistake, and I found out about the consequences of seeking love in all the wrong places. I encourage you to be careful in taking advice from backsliders, because they have the power of persuasion and have no problem sinning. Backsliders are those who continue to sin even though they know that it is wrong to practice ungodly acts. In reality, we need our wounds to heal and our minds to be restored before we enter a new relationship, to avoid bringing in old habits.

I really got myself in some serious trouble playing with fire! I decided to tell God that I was going to sin. I knew that I was going to be punished for sinning, but I was going to take my chances anyway. I was ready to have fun, and I chose to sin and fall into a spirit of lust with romantic poetry. I began to write some romantic works, and that went on for a few years, along with the sin that so easily beset me. I was just having fun, until one day I started experiencing vertigo! I felt like I was walking sideways and was about to fall flat on my face. It was the worst thing that had ever happened to me. My employer called the ambulance, and I was taken out of the building in a wheelchair. I was in the emergency room waiting to find out why I was not able to stand up or keep food in my stomach. The doctors in the emergency room told me that my symptoms were stress related and recommended muscle relaxers. I had to visit my regular doctor to let him know about my experience, and as a result, I took muscle relaxers for several weeks. Then I stopped taking the pills and began drinking Tension Tamer tea to help me relax, because the pills were making me drowsy at work. I realized that I was not able to manage my time well or juggle working full time and tutoring at night. My ultimate problem was that I was sinning before God and everything that was not correct was coming to an end. I was scared and knew that I needed to repent my sins, and God forgave me for sinning. I was glad that God had mercy on me, and I could not stop praising the Lord for delivering me from myself. Amen!

Running from Sin and Running to God

When enough is enough, there is a secret place that you can run to and not become weary. God was trying to get my attention to let me know that He wanted me on His time schedule, because I had too much on my agenda. The Lord wanted me to become devoted to Him and to stop sinning and to concentrate on my salvation. In 2001, I decided that I was going to graduate school, because God had something special for me that year. I started visiting my elderly neighbors and witnessing to them about Jesus. A change had come over me. I had to end my relationships with the people I was seeing, because the hand of the Lord was upon me. I started writing inspirational poetry for a prison ministry newsletter for the church I used to attend. I also began praying and witnessing to the students at school, because I had such a great passion to tell people about Jesus again. I had a testimony to share.

One Sunday morning at church, I heard the Holy Spirit speak to me as I was sitting in the balcony with my mother. It seemed like the voice was so loud, and God spoke to me and said, "I gave power unto you." It was the first time that I heard the voice of God. I was amazed for two weeks and could not share the story with anyone, because I was in shock. The only thing that I could do was say in my heart, *God is almighty, and He does things according to His will*. Months later, God began demonstrating His power mightily in my life. I won scholarships and tutored the class at times. Every Sunday I would meet my mother at church and have breakfast at her house. I was dedicated and blessed to be under divine authority, because God had everything in control. I graduated with honors and was planning to enroll in a doctoral program. Hello, somebody! I felt like I was riding on top of the world and all geared up for the next step in life. I was so puffed up that I started sending out my resume to college institutions to teach in the business field, but God had another plan for my life. The Holy Spirit told me to enroll in a Bible school because I needed to know about God as my Heavenly Father. The thought of attending Bible school was far from my mind, and I had a few months to make a decision before September 2002. I became bored during the waiting period and joined an organization that was geared toward helping minorities. My first choice was to enroll in Bible school and everything else, became secondary. I became a writer for the organization newsletter, and everything seemed like it was working in my favor—until I was tempted by the devil.

The organization was having a fund-raiser aboard a boat on the Hudson River. The event was going to be an all-white affair. I had stopped hanging out that year because I was preparing for the seminary, and the Bible story of Jonah came across my mind. I knew that I was on a quest to change my lifestyle, and the thought of the boat ride was tempting. If I had slipped back into the disco mode and gone on the boat ride, only God knows what would have been in store for me and the people on the boat. Hello, somebody! That was one trap that I was not going to fall into, even though my flesh was fighting against my spirit. I knew that God had something great in store for me, and since I fear God, I started attending classes at a Bible school in Brooklyn. Amen!

The favor of God is what I needed, because some interesting things were happening in my work environment, and I decided to join the poetry club. I had the opportunity to recite some inspirational poetry from the prison ministry newsletter collection. The poetry club was a stepping-stone for me to branch out and to conduct "Inspiration for the Heart and Soul" workshops. God had a plan for me to reach out to the community, and I began to visit senior citizen centers to encourage the men and women at various churches. I spent two years conducting the workshops, and the people were inspired by the words of wisdom that

God inspired me to write. In fact, I am grateful that the Holy Spirit stirred up the gifts inside me to express my faith in God. I believe that God will shape and mold you for whatever task He has prepared for you, and He will not give you more than you can bear. Beloved, harden not your hearts, and learn to be obedient to God.

Living to Please God

I am grateful for God's unmerited favor and the blessings that He has given me. My life has been a continuous journey of ups and downs, needs, and good deeds, but I'm always concerned about making sure everyone that I associate with are doing well. I strongly believe that it is good for me to help others who are in need, regardless of their circumstances, because some people need to be encouraged and are in desperate need to hear a word from the Lord.

During my thirties and forties, I spent a lot of time helping families with their children, and I managed to get things accomplished with just a few hours of my time. I even took the time to spend a couple of days out of the week tutoring children in various subjects. On the weekends, I used to take the children in my family and the neighbors' kids to museums, parks, and Sunday school. I felt that God wanted me to help those in need, and I enjoy seeing a child wearing a smile. There is so much that life has to offer, and my priority has always been to offer my assistance with a grateful heart. I even got the chance to visit some neighbors who were senior men and women before visiting my mother during the week. I used to visit them because many were ill, and I had to tell somebody about Jesus. My neighbors were so excited to talk about Jesus. They enjoyed reading the Bible, praying, and singing Gospel songs. Praise the Lord! I thank God for my strength to do all the deeds that I felt should be done, because life is not all about me.

I have always persevered in the things that I've wanted to accomplish, and my desire is to help others persevere as well. When I hear a person say, "I can't do this" or "I can't see myself doing well," my response is "Let me help you find out what you can do, but ask God for guidance." I believe that people with negative perceptions really have some good qualities lying dormant inside of them, but they need to be motivated to overcome their negative thinking. Based on my experiences in dealing with people, I've found that many have conditioned themselves to think negatively and some have not been able to recognize the accomplishments they have made over the course of their lives. I am not an expert on this subject, but if you are hanging around people who are draining your energy and causing stress, you may consider removing yourself from that crowd.

I have discovered that it is healthier to be in an atmosphere with positive people who can offer you good advice, than to associate yourself with people who are trying to keep you on their level. We need to be endowed with power from God to gain our strength when we are weak. I believe that we desperately need to read and meditate on the Word of God for wisdom. I thank God that I am able to help people who are in need, and I don't take anything for granted, because we are like grass that withers, and the beautiful flowers that fade away. Over the course of my life, I have learned a great deal from men, women, and children. I appreciate the moments we have shared together, because their experiences have helped me to overcome some challenges that could have left me bound in sin. Reading the Word of God has taught me who I am and my purpose in life. I know without a doubt that we were made in the image of God and were born to praise and worship Him in spirit and in truth. I encourage you to embrace the goodness of the Lord and experience the love of God by reading the Bible daily to find out who He really is. God bless you now and always with love and sincerity!

Virtuous

When I look in the mirror, I can see that I have changed. The gray in my hair and the slight wrinkle under my eye are indications that my youth is almost behind me. I feel like I'm growing old, but with wisdom. I'm learning to trust God more than ever before. I've learned from my past mistakes, and I realize that I need to surround myself with positive people who can help nurture me spiritually! I realize that the new journey I desire to take will require patience, willpower, and confidence, and I sincerely trust that God will order my footsteps every step of the way. I will humble myself and stand tall, because my past is behind me. I will be strengthened by the power of the Holy Spirit to handle my present situation, and when I look into the mirror again, I will see a woman who is maturing with grace and is destined to become virtuous!

"I press toward the mark for the prize of the high calling of God in

Christ Jesus." (Philippians 3:14) I pray that you have been encouraged and inspired by these words of wisdom to live a virtuous and humble life. Embrace the love of God and rejoice in the Word. His mercy endures forever!

The Author can be contacted via e-mail at aginspire@aol.com.